Slow Cooker

100% Vegan Indian

Tantalizing and Super Nutritious Vegan Recipes for Optimal Health

By Karen Greenvang

Copyright ©Karen Greenvang 2016

other qualified health professionals regarding the treatment of medical conditions. The author shall not be held liable or responsible for any misunderstanding or misuse of the information contained in this book. The information is not intended to diagnose, treat or cure any disease.

It is important to remember that the author of this book is not a doctor/ medical professional. Only opinions based upon her own personal experiences or research are cited. THE AUTHOR DOES NOT OFFER MEDICAL ADVICE or prescribe any treatments. For any health or medical issues – you should be talking to your doctor first.

Contents

Introduction

Thank you so much for taking an interest in my recipes. It really means a lot to me!

This small recipe book is all about delicious vegan slow cooker recipes from the Indian subcontinent.

Since ancient times, food has been revered for its healing properties, be it emotional or physical. This stands especially true for the Indian culinary tradition where each ingredient in a meal has a healing role aside from keeping the taste buds happy.

Whether its cumin, coriander, red chili, black pepper, cardamom, clove, or mango powder, each spice has a unique healing property that makes it valuable in the food we eat. Some are known for their anti-inflammatory properties, others for aiding in digestion, and many for boosting immunity. The amount of specific spices used in a recipe is directly related to the main ingredients used in that recipe. For example, lentils, which are rich in protein, require a more generous amount of cloves, black cardamom, and ginger, whereas light and watery vegetables can be cooked with or without these spices. Most vegetables only need a very gentle showering of spices.

Regional cuisines

One thing that sets the Indian cuisine apart from others is the fact that it has been evolving for more than 5,000 years. Since the subcontinent was always invaded by one of the other groups of people from around the world who subsequently made it their home, you will see a vast variety of food habits in this region that were not originally a part of the Indus civilization. Wheat, barley, rice, corn, lentils, chickpeas, potatoes, tomatoes, onions, garlic, ginger, asafoetida, mustard, cloves, black pepper, and cayenne pepper – you name it, and it is being used in some form in this diverse country.

Talking about diversity, just because India enjoys a wide variety of religious and cultural lifestyles, you can see the miscellany in culinary practices as well. From one region or religion to another, or one culture to another, there can be varying practices. Many religious groups like Jains and Brahmins do not consume onion or garlic, and eating meat or fish is akin to committing sin. Many communities do not eat root vegetables like potatoes, onions, or tubers. The diversity in food also owes to the range of climates and topography enjoyed in the country. When it is snowing in the north, the people in the south are still sweating from the heat.

India has also had a rich tradition of "slow cooking" in earthen pots. That culinary practice has changed dramatically over the last 50 years. As more women join the workforce or pursue active social lives, pressure cooking technology has gained easy acceptance. Most lentils and vegetables are now cooked within 10-25 minutes in a pressure cooker. While pressure cooker stays the preferred way of cooking nowadays, the slow cooking methods of "angeethi," "kachi rasoi," "chulha," and tandoor are still revered as the authentic and healthy cooking styles.

Let's look at a few of these spices and the healing value they bring to the foods they are cooked in. As you glance at the recipes in the pages ahead, you will see how they enhance the flavors of the meals.

a) Turmeric: The bright yellow powder has come to symbolize Indian cuisine. It is made out of the dried underground stem of a ginger-like plant which is native to India, but grown all across the world. In the Indian healing tradition, it is considered to have a warming effect on the body and is often used as medicine to treat injuries, inflammation, cold, and infection. Turmeric is considered to be an anticancer agent because of a chemical it contains called "curcumin." It adds the magical yellowish-orange color to savory Indian recipes along with a strong taste and aroma that adds to the appeal of the meal.

b) Cumin seeds: These tiny dry seeds are native to India and the Mediterranean region and are extensively cultivated and consumed in India. These seeds form the basis of Indian cuisine and provide it a distinct flavor. They are high in fat and fiber and are known to aid in digestion.

c) Coriander: Coriander, or cilantro, is a very popular herb in many continents across the globe – South Asia, Africa and Europe. Mexican, Burmese, and Indian cuisine rely heavily on the seeds as well as leaves in their cooking. Fresh leaves are ideal for garnishing and enhancing flavor. Coriander is a very nutritious herb. Its leaves are exceptionally rich in Vitamin A, C and K. The seeds are good sources of iron, calcium, selenium and dietary fiber. The herb is known to help calm irritable bowel syndrome and has an antianxiety effect. It has been shown to lower cholesterol as well.

d) Red chili: Red chili belongs to the pepper family. In Indian cuisine, it is used as dry whole pepper as well as in powder form. They are known to have originated in Mexico and then traveled the world over. They provide a spicy flavor to any cuisine and offer anti-inflammatory and antioxidant benefits. The good news for people on weight loss programs is that consuming red chili helps metabolism by making the body burn fat faster.

e) Black cardamom: Also known as Indian cardamom or Bengal cardamom, the seeds have a camphor-like aroma and stronger cardamom flavor. Black cardamom is reserved for savory dishes while the green one is mostly used in sweet dishes. It goes very well with rice and protein-rich foods like chickpeas, lentils, and green leafy vegetables like spinach. Black cardamom is very effective in treating gastrointestinal disorders including heartburn and stomach cramps. It helps keep your heart healthy and improves skin and hair.

f) Cloves: This tiny black spice is native to the Maluku Islands in Indonesia, but is consumed and harvested in India, Pakistan, Sri Lanka, and Bangladesh, among other countries. This reddish-black dried flower bud of the evergreen clove tree resembles a nail in its shape. Its anti-inflammatory and anti-oxidant properties are very well-known. Other than its ability to fight bacteria, it also has a numbing effect, which makes it a popular remedy for toothaches.

g) Asafoetida: A form of dry latex that originated in Persia and spread to South Asia, asafoetida has a strong and pungent taste and aroma. It aids in digestion and supports healthy respiratory and nervous function. It should always be fried before being added to food and used in moderation.

Breakfast

Oatmeal Daliya

Daliya is a popular breakfast for Indians and is satiating and nutritious. Indians are fond of using milk and milk-products in their culinary preparations. The original recipe calls for milk (sadly), however (luckily), it can easily be substituted with almond milk. Here is our vegan version of the traditional daliya cooked in a slow cooker. Vegan is better!

Servings: 2

Preparation Time: 00H:03M:00
Cooking time: 08H:0M:00
Total Time: 08H:3M:00

INGREDIENTS:

- Steel-cut oatmeal: 1 cup
- Almond milk: Three cups
- Raisins: 2 tbsp.
- Pistachios: 1 tablespoon
- Cardamom: 4 pods
- Brown or coconut Sugar: 1 tablespoon

COOKING INSTRUCTIONS:

1. For a hot steaming oatmeal daliya for breakfast, start cooking at night, preferably around 10 pm.

2. Grind cardamom pods and seeds together finely.

3. Switch on the slow cooker.

4. Throw the oatmeal into the slow cooker along with cardamom powder, pistachios, and raisins as the cooker starts to warm up. Stir well for 2-3 minutes.

5. Add almond milk and sugar.

6. Leave the slow cooker at low, heat overnight for 8 hours.

7. Wake up in the morning to the Indian-style, gluten-free, vegan oatmeal daliya. Enjoy the delicate flavor of cardamom and pistachios.

Rice Kheer

Kheer, a type of rice pudding, is a very popular dessert in Indian cuisine. There are different ways of cooking this rice pudding, and luckily, vegan milk can replace the milk as required in the original recipe. You can also choose which nuts to use, or omit them in the recipe as per your taste and eating habits.

Servings: 4

Preparation Time: 00H:10M:00
Cooking time: 08H:0M:00
Total Time: 08H:10M:00

INGREDIENTS

- Long-grain rice (basmati is preferred): ¾ Cup
- Vegan milk (almond or coconut milk): 5 Cups
- Coconut or brown Sugar: 1/4 Cup
- Coconut oil: 1 tbsp. + 1tbsp.
- Cardamom: 4 pods
- Raisins : 20
- Chopped nuts : ½ cup
- Saffron: 4-5 strands

COOKING INSTRUCTIONS:

1. Wash the rice thoroughly under running water until the water runs clear. Set it aside.

2. Coat the inner sides and bottom of the ceramic pot of the slow cooker with 1 tablespoon of coconut oil. Switch on the slow cooker and set it to medium.

3. Run the cardamom through a coffee grinder until it reaches a fine powdery consistency.

4. Combine rice, vegan milk, sugar, and cardamom powder. Pour into the slow cooker and set the heat to low.

5. Make sure that your slow cooker is at least half to three fourths full.

6. Stir the rice and milk every half hour so that the rice does not stick to the bottom of the ceramic pot.

7. Meanwhile, in a small shallow frying pan, add 1 tablespoon of coconut oil and roast the chopped cashews, pistachios, and almonds over low heat for about a minute or two until fragrant. The chopped nuts will turn a light brown color.

8. The length of cooking time depends on the size and make of your cooker. If it is a 3-quart cooker, it should take 8 hours.

9. After about 6 hours of cooking, add the roasted nuts along with the raisins. Mix thoroughly and cook for

another two hours until the rice has reached a thick consistency and the grains have softened.

10. You can either serve it hot or leave it to cool down for an hour and then keep it in the fridge for around 4 hours until it's chilled. Garnish with saffron strands on top. Saffron will add authentic Indian flavor and aroma to this rice pudding.

Tizann

Tizann is a Goan porridge made out of ragi, or finger millet. It is not only vegan, but also gluten-free and very nutritious. Ragi is a nutrition-packed grain that is high in iron and calcium and very beneficial in healing wounds. It is a popular breakfast in central and southern India.

Servings: 2

Preparation time: 04H.25M:00
Cooking time: 03H:00M:00
Total time: 07H:25M:00

INGREDIENTS:

- Finger millet: 1 cup
- Water: 2 cups
- Coconut chunks : 1 cup
- Palm jaggery: 2 tbsp. or more to taste
- Salt: 1 pinch
- Cashew nuts: 4
- Raisins: 8

COOKING INSTRUCTIONS:

1. Wash the millet under running water in a fine wire mesh. Soak it in warm water for 4 hours.
2. Grind millet with coconut and ½ cup water.
3. Add one cup water and stir well.
4. Pour the mixture into a muslin cloth and extract the juice into a bowl.
5. Add ground jaggery into the juice with a pinch of salt.
6. Pour the mixture into a slow cooker and cook it at low heat for 3 hours. Stir it a few times in between, ensuring the mixture doesn't get burnt.
7. Once the mixture starts to thicken, turn off the slow cooker.
8. Chop cashew nuts into small pieces.
9. Serve the ragi porridge or Tizann hot, garnished with chopped cashew nuts and raisins.

Pav Bhaji

Pav Bhaji is a popular Maharashtrian dish that can be eaten for any meal. It is a spicy vegetable medley that is nutritious and filling. It is eaten with bread called paav that is popular in India. Paav can be attributed to the English-Portuguese influence over Indian cuisine. You can substitute paav with gluten-free or cornmeal bread.

Most Indian recipes call for a tempering, or "tarka." In this recipe, it's important to prepare the tempering beforehand and add it to the slow cooker. Assuming your slow cooker has limited functions, this recipe provides tempering steps in a frying pan.

Servings: 2

Preparation time: 00H.30M:00
Cooking time: 03H:00M:00
Total time: 03H:30M:00

INGREDIENTS:

- Potatoes: 4 medium-sized
- Tomatoes: 2 medium-sized

- Cauliflower florets: 1 cup
- Green peas: ½ cup
- Green bell peppers: 1 medium-sized
- Onions: 2 medium-sized
- Garlic: 3 cloves
- Ginger: 1 inch piece
- Fresh Coriander: ½ cup
- Chili powder: ¼ tbsp.
- Salt: 1 tbsp.
- Dry coriander powder: 2 tbsp.
- Cumin seeds: 1 tbsp.
- Dry mango powder: 1 tbsp.
- Oil: 2 tbsp.
- Vegan Margarine: 4 tbsp.
- Water: 2 cups
- Lemons: 2 small sized

COOKING INSTRUCTIONS:

Prepare tempering:

1. Chop onions, garlic, ginger, tomatoes, and bell pepper finely, then set aside.
2. Heat 2 tablespoons of oil in a frying pan on medium heat.
3. Lower the heat once the oil has warmed up. Add cumin seeds and wait until they start to crackle, then add

coriander powder and curry leaves. Sauté for one minute.

4. Next, add chopped onion, garlic, and ginger mixture and let it fry until light brown. This should take approximately 7-10 minutes.

5. Add chopped tomatoes and mix well with the fried paste. Cover with a lid and let it cook for 5-7 minutes. Add chili and dried mango powder and mix it well. Let it cook for another minute.

6. Remove the lid and check to see if the tomatoes are well-cooked and blended. The mixture should be a nice reddish paste.

7. Let it cook uncovered until the water evaporates completely and the mixture starts to pull away from the bottom of the pan. You will know that the tempering or "tarka" is ready when the oil starts to separate from the mixture.

8. Add chopped bell pepper and let it cook for 3 minutes.

9. Turn off the heat, add a spoonful of vegan margarine, cover with a lid, and set aside.

Preparing the bhaaji:

1. Peel potatoes and cut into 1"x1"cubes.
2. Cut cauliflower into small florets.
3. Switch on the slow cooker and set to medium heat.

4. Pour in 2 cups of water and add potatoes, peas, and cauliflower. Add the fried tempering mixture followed by another spoonful of vegan margarine.
5. Let the curry cook for 3 hours until the veggies are soft. Use a potato masher to lightly mash the veggies to create the texture of a very thick stew.
6. Turn off the slow cooker. The curry is ready!

SERVING SUGGESTIONS:

1. Garnish the curry with finely chopped fresh coriander leaves. Serve with another spoonful of vegan margarine on top.
2. This curry is popularly eaten with Indian baked buns called paav, which are not gluten-free.
3. To keep this meal gluten-free, substitute the buns with gluten-free or cornmeal bread. The paav is traditionally toasted on "tawa," or a skillet, with some oil or vegan margarine.
4. Serve this meal with lemon slices that can be squeezed on the bhaaji or curry. A few drops of lemon can enhance the flavor.

Spicy Barley Chaat

Chats are a popular snack in India, and they can be found in a huge variety, for example papdi chat, tiki chat, bhelpuri chat, fruit chat, aalu chat, dahi bada chat, and so forth. We have tweaked the usual bhelpuri chat to a more nutritious, vegan, and gluten-free recipe that will be a great start to the day. Barley is high in fiber and has a huge range of vitamins and minerals like selenium, manganese, phosphorous, and niacin.

Servings: 4

Preparation Time: 00H:15M:00
Cooking Time: 08H:00M:00
Total time: 08H:15M:00

- 1 cup pot or pearl barley
- Water: 4 ½ cups
- Lightly fried peanuts: ½ cup
- Coriander: ¼ cup
- Tomato: 1 medium-sized
- Green chili : 1, mild
- Frozen corn: ½ cup
- Potato: 1 medium-sized
- Tamarind chutney: 2 tbsp.
- Salt: 1 tsp.

- Lemon: 1 tbsp. juice

COOKING INSTRUCTIONS:

1. Rinse barley thoroughly under running water.
2. Switch on your 3-quart slow cooker at medium setting.
3. Add water, one cup barley, and salt.
4. Leave it in the slow cooker for 6 hours.
5. Chop potatoes and thaw the frozen corn. Rinse both and throw into the cooker, let it cook for 2 hours.
6. Meanwhile, chop tomatoes, coriander, and green chilies.
7. Empty slow cooker contents into a serving bowl. Add the chopped veggies along with tamarind chutney and salt. Mix well.
8. Add fried peanuts (with skins) and mix well. Sprinkle lemon on top and garnish with finely-chopped coriander. You can serve it at room temperature or refrigerate it for half an hour to eat it chilled.

Bajre Ka Khichda

Bajra, or black millet, is a staple food of north-western Rajasthan, a semi-arid region of the subcontinent. This grain is highly nutritious and especially strong in iron and fiber. Bajre ka khichda is a very popular traditional food of the Rajasthanis. It is filling and considered a "warm food." Hence, it is mostly consumed during the winter season. The locals in the region like to make flatbreads and desserts out of black millet flour, a gluten-free, non-GMO grain that is relatively easy to cook.

Serving: 2

Preparation time: 00:05:00
Cooking time: 04H:00M:00
Total time: 04H:05M:00

INGREDIENTS:

- Black millet: 1 cup
- Coconut oil: 1 tbsp.
- Coconut jaggery: ¼ cup
- Salt: 1/8 tsp.
- Walnuts: 4
- Raisins: 8
- Almonds: 4
- Makhane (dried lotus stem): 10

COOKING INSTRUCTIONS:

1. Heat a small frying pan over a medium flame.
2. As the pan warms up, add coconut oil and let it heat.
3. Throw a cup of black millet grains into the pan and stir them continuously for 5 minutes.
4. After five minutes, remove the pan from the stove. Let it cool for a few minutes.
5. Meanwhile, set up the slow cooker on low heat.
6. Add 4 cups of water and salt into the cooker.
7. Throw in the lightly sautéed millet grains.
8. After 3 hours, add makhane, almonds, raisins, walnuts, and jaggery. Continue cooking.
9. After 1 hour, switch off the cooker. Transfer the cooked millet into a bowl and serve hot.

Indian cuisine uses ghee in most of its recipes. Ghee is made out of butter. For a vegan diet, we recommend using coconut oil. Sweet recipes won't taste right with any other oil.

Using a 3 quart slow cooker would be ideal for the amount cooked in this recipe.

Lunch

Palak Tofu Curry

Palak paneer is a celebrated dish of north India and is offered at most restaurants and feasts. It is mostly popular because of the inclusion of "paneer," a kind of cheese that resembles feta, though not as strong in flavor. Paneer is a rather expensive food item and is mostly prepared for guests or special occasions. We have adapted this recipe for vegans and replaced paneer with tofu. Although tofu isn't originally from India, it has rapidly found its place in Indian restaurants and culinary books. Since Chinese cuisine is quite popular in India, it is not difficult to find tofu at most supermarkets. When cooking this recipe, look for extra-firm tofu.

This dish is nutritious, combining calcium and protein-rich tofu with the goodness of spinach.

Servings: 4

Preparation time: 00H:10M:00
Cooking time: 02H:10M:00
Total Time: 02H:20M:00

INGREDIENTS:

- Spinach leaves: 4 cups
- Extra firm tofu: 1 block/tub (300 grams)
- Tomato: 1 medium-sized
- Onion: 1 medium-sized
- Ginger: 2"x2" piece
- Garlic: 2 cloves
- Salt: 1 tsp.
- Cumin seeds: 1 tsp.
- Chili powder: 1 tsp.
- Cloves: 2
- Black cardamom: 1 pod
- Cinnamon stick: 1 inch
- Coriander powder: 1 tbsp.
- Dried mango powder: 1 tsp.
- Coconut oil: 2 tbsp.
- Water: 2 cups

COOKING INSTRUCTIONS:

1. Blanch the spinach leaves in two cups of water in a small pan for 3-4 minutes. Drain the spinach and save the water to reuse later when preparing the

curry. The water holds many nutrients from the spinach.

2. Puree the spinach with tomato and set aside.

3. Grind onions, ginger, and garlic into a smooth paste.

4. Heat a frying pan and add 2 tablespoons of oil. Add cumin seeds. As they begin to crackle, add coriander powder. Sauté for 30 seconds. Add onion, ginger, and garlic paste. Sauté until light brown and the mixture starts to leave the bottom of the pan. This must be done on low heat for approximately 5-7 minutes.

5. Now, add the sautéed paste into the slow cooker along with pureed spinach and tomato. Add the leftover water from the spinach, chili powder, dried mango powder, cardamom, and cinnamon stick along with the cloves.

6. Switch on the slow cooker to low and let it cook for 2 hours. After it has been cooked for 1.5 hours, throw in the tofu cubes and let it cook for another half hour.

7. The delicious spinach curry is ready with all the aromatic flavors of the Indian subcontinent.

8. This curry is mostly eaten with Indian flatbread or rice. If you eat it with rice, your meal becomes 100% vegan and gluten-free!

Sarson da Saag and Makki di Roti

Sarson, or mustard, is a popular food in Punjab, the Western fertile plains of India, which were known as the bread basket of the country for the longest time. Sarson is grown in the winter, and a pureed form of this leafy vegetable is coupled with cornmeal flat bread, making it a staple diet of the hard-working Punjabis.

This meal is totally vegan and gluten-free. It's a highly nutritious meal as mustard greens are known to have high vitamin and beta-carotene content as well as other minerals like calcium and manganese.

Servings: 4

Preparation time:01H:00:00

Cooking time: 08:00:00

Total time: 09:00:00

INGREDIENTS:

- Mustard greens: 4 cups
- Spinach: 2 cups
- Onion: 1 medium-sized
- Garlic: 2 cloves
- Ginger: 2" x 2" piece
- Green chilies: 1

- Coriander powder: 1 tbsp.
- Salt: 1 tbsp. or more per taste
- Vegan Margarine: 2 tbsp.
- Coconut Oil: 2 tbsp.
- Water: 6 cups

COOKING INSTRUCTIONS:

1. Wash the mustard greens and spinach leaves thoroughly and chop them finely.
2. Switch on the slow cooker and set to low heat. Throw in the greens along with 6 cups of water. Let them cook for 6 hours.
3. Chop onions, garlic, ginger, and chilies.
4. Heat up a frying pan and add 2 tbsp. of oil. When the oil is hot, add cumin seeds.
5. After one minute, the seeds will begin to sizzle. Add chopped onions, garlic, and ginger, and sauté it for 7-8 minutes on medium heat.
6. Once the mixture turns brown, add coriander powder and stir well.
7. After 30 seconds, add chopped chilies and cover the lid for 2 minutes. Keep over low flame.
8. Remove the frying pan from the stove and pour the mixture into the slow cooker with the cooked greens. Stir the entire

mixture to combine. Let the flavours of the sautéed veggies blend with the greens.

9. Continue cooking for another hour. Make sure to add another cup of water if the greens are too dry. The entire curry must have a gravy-like consistency.

10. After one hour, switch off the cooker and pour the contents into a large serving bowl. Blend with a hand blender for 2 minutes to ensure the green mustard curry has a pureed consistency. If it's watery, let it cook for another hour to make sure the water evaporates and thick gravy remains.

11. My French friend likes to add asparagus or Brussels sprouts to it. Once you get a knack for cooking this highly nutritious antioxidant rich green curry, you can add a few other veggies of your choice for more of a nutty flavor to enrich this dish and suit your palate.

12. Serve the mustard curry hot with two spoons of vegan margarine. Traditionally, this dish is topped with homemade white butter, but since we are keeping this vegan, we will substitute it with vegan margarine. Cornmeal flatbread is eaten with this curry.

Cabbage Potato Curry

This is one of those curries that cooks quickly and is very nutritious, packed with vitamin A, B, C, and K, and a vast range of minerals and dietary fiber. Cabbage is more or less a flavourless vegetable. In this recipe, the spices lend a delicious flavour and appetizing aroma to the otherwise bland potato and cabbage combination.

Servings: 4

Preparation Time: 00H:20M:00
Cooking Time: 04H:00M:00
Total Time: 04H:20M:00

INGREDIENTS

- Cabbage: 1 medium head
- Potatoes: 3 medium-sized
- Coconut oil: 2 tbsp.
- Garlic: 2 cloves
- Ginger: ½ tsp.
- Onions: 2 large
- Turnip white: 2 medium
- Turmeric: ½ tsp.
- Cumin seeds: ½ tsp.
- Bay leaves : 1

- Salt : ¾ teaspoon
- Ground black pepper: 1/8 tsp.
- Fresh coriander leaves: 2 tbsp.
- Water : ½ cup

COOKING INSTRUCTIONS:

1. Grind onions, ginger, and garlic to a paste.
2. Slice cabbage lengthwise.
3. Chop coriander leaves finely.
4. Peel potatoes and white turnips. Dice them into small cubes.
5. Spray the inside of the crock pot with coconut oil and switch it on. Throw in cumin seeds, turmeric, and coriander powder. Sautee it until the cumin seeds start to crackle. Add ginger garlic paste. Let it cook for 15 minutes in the oil until it turns golden.
6. Add salt, black pepper, and bay leaf. Add potato, turnip, and water and let it cook for 3 hours.
7. After 3 hours, throw in the cabbage, stir it well, and continue cooking for another hour.
8. After 4 hours of cooking, your cabbage curry is ready.
9. Serve hot with a topping of freshly chopped coriander.

Aalu Matar Sabji

Who doesn't like potatoes? They are rich in carbs and many minerals, a good source of Vitamin B6, and best of all, they are comfort food to most people. Although potato was not a native vegetable to Indians for a long time, today it is a very popular ingredient in many Indian meals. The best part about potatoes is that you can combine them with so many different ingredients - spices, vegetables etc. Be it basil in Italy, cumin in India, potato rocks everywhere!

This curry is a combination of potatoes with green peas in gravy cooked with onion, ginger, and tomatoes and a variety of spices.

Servings: 4

Preparation time: 00H:20M:00
Cooking time: 04H:20M:00
Total time: 04H:20M:00
INGREDIENTS:

- Potatoes: 3
- Peas: 2 cups
- Tomatoes: 3 medium-sized
- Onions: 2 medium-sized
- Coconut oil: 1 tbsp.
- Ginger-Garlic paste: 1 ½ tsp.
- Green Chilies: 2

- Turmeric: 1 tsp.
- Red chili powder: ½ tsp.
- Coriander powder: ½ tsp.
- Cumin seeds: 1 tsp.
- Salt: 1 tsp.
- Fresh coriander leaves: 1/4 cup
- Water: 1 cup

COOKING INSTRUCTIONS:

1. Wash the potatoes under warm running water. Peel and dice the potatoes into 1 inch cube size. Set aside in a bowl full of cold water.
2. Finely chop onions and tomatoes. Next, grind ginger, garlic, and green chilies to a paste.
3. Heat up a frying pain on the stove and pour 1 tbsp. coconut oil.
4. Once the oil warms up, add cumin seeds. Fry for 2 minutes. Add turmeric and coriander powder and fry for 15 seconds.
5. Add ginger-garlic paste and fry for 3 minutes.
6. Add chopped onion and sauté for 5 minutes.
7. Finally, add chopped tomatoes and all the dry ingredients.

8. Once it is well-cooked, you will notice the paste starts to leave the bottom of the pan and the oil separates from the paste. Now, it is time to add the potato cubes and peas. Stir for 2 minutes until well combined.

9. Set up the crock pot and add the contents of the frying pan into the pot. Add 1 cup of water. The crock pot must at least be half full.

10. Cook for 4 hours on high. Check after four hours to see if it requires any more cooking. Insert a fork into the dish to check if the potatoes are well-cooked.

11. Once done, garnish with chopped cilantro and serve hot with flatbread.

Sambhar Daal

Pigeon peas in a mouth-watering tamarind-based spicy curry or "sambhar" as it is popularly called is a popular main course in Southern states in India, but its popularity has traveled far and wide. Sambhar can be considered as a lentil-based chowder that uses tamarind and curry leaves to add a distinct flavour to these ordinary lentils.

Cooking suggestion: If you have a traditional slow cooker with limited functions, then it is a good idea to prepare "tarka," or shallow frying the spicy base of the sambhar separately in a pan. This recipe offers the details on preparing a separate "tarka."

Serves: 4
Preparation Time: 00H:20M:00
Cooking Time: 04H:00M:00
Total Time: 04H:20M:00

INGREDIENTS:
- Arhar (Toovar) Lentils: 1 cup
- Drumsticks: 12 inches long (2)
- Onions: 1 medium-sized
- Curry leaves: 12 leaves
- Tamarind paste: 1 tbsp.
- Cumin seeds: ½ tsp.

- Ground Coriander powder: 1 tsp.
- Asofoetida (Hing): ⅙ tsp.
- Fenugreek seeds: ½ tsp.
- Mustard seeds: ½ tsp.
- Turmeric powder: 1 tsp.
- Coconut oil: 1 ½ tbsp.
- Grated coconut powder: 1 tbsp.
- Red chilies, whole: 2
- Water: 3 ½ cups

COOKING INSTRUCTIONS:

1. Wash arhar daal or lentils thoroughly in running water until the water drains clear. Let them soak for 10 minutes.
2. Wash drumsticks and curry leaves in running water.
3. Cut drumsticks into 2 inches pieces and set aside.
4. Wipe off the water drops and moisture from curry leaves by rubbing them in a paper towel.
5. Chop onions into medium-sized pieces.
6. Take one tablespoon of tamarind paste and stir it in half cup hot water until it dissolves.
7. Set up the slow cooker and add 4 cups water, arhar daal, and drumsticks.

8. Heat up a frying pan at medium setting on the stove.

9. Pour coconut oil into the pan and let it heat for 3 minutes on medium.

10. Add cumin seeds, and once they start sizzling, add asafoetida and fenugreek seeds. Fry for 5 minutes until the seeds turn light brown.

11. Add red chilies, mustard seeds, coriander powder, and curry leaves. Let them fry for 2 minutes. Add chopped onions and fry for 3-4 minutes until lightly cooked. Do not let them turn brown. Turn off the stove.

12. Add this fried mixture into the slow cooker along with the grated coconut powder. Let it cook for 3 hours.

13. After 3 hours, remove the lid and add tamarind and water paste. Let it cook for another hour as the flavours of the different spices and the tamarind are infused into each lentil grain and a tangy-flavoured sambhar is ready.

14. You can eat it with idli, dosa, wadaa, or rice, which are all gluten-free and go very well with Sambhar.

Idli

If you decided to make Sambhar, eating it with idli is the next best thing you can do to enjoy the flavourful lentil curry. Idli is more or less a rice cake that is really low in calories as it has almost no fat other than a drop of oil for each little cake. It is steamed and hence very light on the digestion. Teaming it with Sambhar makes it a wholesome meal as you get your proteins from lentils, vitamins and minerals from the veggies and spices in the curry, and your carbs from idlis.

The best part about idlis is that you can make one batch of 20-30 and store them in the fridge for 4-5 days, or just freeze them. We have provided some "re-use" suggestions for idli at the end of this recipe.

Servings: 5 (5 idlis per serving)

Preparation Time: 15H:00M:00
Cooking Time: 00H:40M:00
Total time: 15H:40M:00

INGREDIENTS:

- Parboiled rice: 1 cup
- Split black lentils (urad daal): ¼ cup
- Fenugreek seeds: ½ tsp.

- Salt: 1 tsp.
- Coconut oil: 2 tbsp.
- Water: 1 ¼ cup
- Idli-maker required. If you don't have one, you can use a small muffin tray, although they won't be quite as fluffy when steamed in a muffin tray.

COOKING INSTRUCTIONS:

1. Rinse split black lentils and fenugreek seeds under running water until the drained water is clear. Soak them in clean water, cover with a lid, and set aside for four hours.
2. Rinse two cups of rice grains in running water until the drained water is clear. Soak them in clean water, cover with a lid, and set aside for four hours.
3. After four hours, drain the water from the lentils and fenugreek seeds and rinse them again.
4. Add the contents into a blender with ½ cup water and run the blender for 4 minutes, just enough to get a smooth paste. It should be a slightly grainy paste, not as smooth as an all-purpose flour batter.

5. Wash and drain the parboiled rice and rinse it once. Run it in the blender for 4 minutes with ¾ cup water to ensure the batter is on the thicker side.

6. Combine the lentil batter with the rice batter. Add salt and stir well so the contents are well mixed. Cover it with a tight lid and let it sit for 12 hours in a warm place. During this time, fermentation will take place. Stir it a few times while it ferments.

7. After 12 hours when the batter is well-fermented, it is now ready to be steamed into idlis.

8. Heat up your multi-cooker or rice cooker and switch it to STEAM settings.

9. Place one quart of water in the cooking pot. If you don't have idli maker, insert a steaming rack for the muffin tray. Press STEAM. Set desired cooking time to 1 hour. The cooker will get into preheat mode, and as soon as the exact temperature for steaming is reached, it will indicate through a light or beep.

10. Meanwhile, grease the idli maker or muffin tray with a drop of coconut oil in each cup. Pour idli batter into the cups. Once your steamer is ready, place the tray on the steaming rack. If using an idli maker, it can go directly into the steaming cooker.

11. Let it cook for one hour. The cooker will stop automatically after an hour. Let it rest for 5 minutes and remove the lid.

12. Check the idlis with a fork. If the fork comes out clean and the idlis look like firm rice cakes, remove the idli-maker. If the fork comes out with batter stuck to it, they will require another half hour of steaming.

13. Enjoy these warm idlis with sambhar curry or simple coconut chutney.

14. What if you are left with idlis after dinner? Here's how you can enjoy your leftover idlis:

   -Warm up idlis in a microwave or leave at room temperature for a couple of hours. Eat them with sambhar or any other curry.
   -"Idli-fry" for breakfast or a snack!

Prepare a tempering of coconut oil, salt, curry leaves, cumin, and mustard seeds in a frying pan. Add a pinch of red chili powder. Dice idlis into cubes and throw them into the frying pan after the tempering is ready. Make sure that each idli is coated in some of the tempering by flipping them in the pan a few times. Sprinkle a few drops of water on the diced idlis. Cover the pan for 3 minutes. Your "idli-fry" is ready for a quick spicy breakfast or snack!

Chana Masala

Chana masala is a scrumptious main course for any north Indian feast. It is popularly combined with fried breads like poori or bhaturas. Chana, or chick peas, are very popular in India. High in protein and fiber, chick peas are also an excellent source of minerals like manganese, folate, copper, and phosphorous. They are considered an excellent ingredient to add to your meal if you are aiming for healthy weight loss.

Servings: 4

Preparation time: 04H:20M:00
Cooking time: 08H:00:00
Total time: 08H:20M:00

INGREDIENTS:

- Chick peas: 2 cups
- Tomatoes: 2 medium
- Onion: 1 medium
- Ginger: 2"x2"
- Fresh coriander: ¼ cup
- Tamarind paste: 1 tbsp.
- Himalayan salt: 1 tsp.
- Black salt: 1 tsp.

- Red chili: ¼ tsp.
- Lightly roasted cumin powder: 1 tsp.
- Lightly roasted coriander powder: 2 tbsp.
- Cloves: 2
- Black cardamom: 2 large pods
- Dried bay leaf: 2
- Coconut oil: 1 tbsp.
- Water: 4 cups to soak/3 cups to cook

COOKING INSTRUCTION:

1. Rinse chick peas seven to nine times under running water, making sure you rub the beans between your hands before draining. According to traditional Indian cooking, this steps ensures easy digestion of the protein-rich lentils.

2. Soak chick peas in water for four hours after adding ½ spoon of black rock salt.

3. Switch on the slow cooker when the beans have been soaked for four hours, and you are ready to start cooking.

4. Set your slow cooker's heat to high and add one tablespoon of coconut oil. Throw in the chick peas with all the dry ingredients listed above. Cover with a lid.

5. Meanwhile, slice the onions into halves. Rest the onion with the cut side down on the chopping board. With a

sharp knife, start slicing along the lines of longitude, from top end to root end. Slice both of the onions in this manner and keep the long strands in a bowl.

6. Chop ginger, tomatoes, and coriander and add them to the bowl with the onions.

7. Add the contents of the veggie bowl into the slow cooker.

8. Set the timer for the chana masala to cook for eight hours.

9. As soon as the timer goes off, remove the lid to check if the peas are cooked and easy to mash with a fork. The rest of the ingredients should have broken down into a tempting curry. Add the tamarind paste and stir well into the curry. Let it sit for another half hour. At this time, you can also check the flavor of the curry. If you want to add chilies or salt, or add some water to make it into thinner gravy, do it now. You can let it boil for another 15-20 minutes or just let it sit to cook further in its steam.

10. Serve hot, garnished with chopped fresh coriander leaves and flat bread.

Dinner

Mahni Soup

Mahni is a Kashmiri delight, a raw mango soup that is great to start any festive dinner. This is a rather simple but tangy soup that offers the best of the flavours of the royal fruit, mango, infused with onions and chili.

Mango is high in potassium and rich in flavour.

Servings: 4

Preparation time: 00H30M:00
Cooking Time: 03H:00:00
Total time: 03H:30M:00

INGREDIENTS:

- Ripe or half-ripe mangoes: 2
- Onion: 1 small
- Mint leaves: ½ cup
- Coriander leaves: 2 tbsp.
- Himalayan salt: 1 tsp.
- Black pepper: ¼ tsp.
- Cumin seed powder (roasted): ½ tsp.
- Red chili flakes: ⅛ tsp.

- Brown or coconut Sugar: 2 tsp.
- Water: 3½ cups

COOKING INSTRUCTIONS:

1. Wash the mangoes thoroughly.
2. Switch on the slow cooker to the low setting. Add 2 cups of water. Add the raw mangoes and let them cook gently for 3 hours.
3. After 3 hours, remove the mangoes and set them aside to cool for a while.
4. Peel the skin, separate the pulp into a bowl and run it through a blender.
5. Chop the onion, mint, and coriander leaves finely and add it to the mango pulp.
6. Now add the dry spices, salt, and sugar along with 1½ cups of boiling water.
7. Stir the mixture well and serve it hot.

Kidney Bean Curry

Rajmah-chawal or mothi chawal as they are popularly known in North-west India is the combination of red kidney bean curry and rice. This is a protein, iron, and carb-rich dish that can best be categorized as comfort food for most youngsters. The onion-tomato-ginger base makes it delicious and enhances the flavour of the kidney beans. You can cook a large pot of this and then freeze it in portions of 1 or 2 servings. Whenever you want to eat kidney bean curry, just cook some fresh rice, defrost and heat up this curry, and you will have a delicious, vegan, gluten-free meal ready within minutes!

Servings: 10

Preparation time: 00H:10M:00
Cooking time: 08:00M:00
Total time: 08H:10M:00

Ingredients:
- Red kidney beans: 1½ cups
- Tomatoes: 2 medium
- Onion: 1 medium
- Ginger: 2"x2"
- Garlic : 4 cloves
- Fresh coriander: ¼ cup

- Dried fenugreek leaves: 2 tbsp.
- Red chili: ¼ tsp.
- Lightly roasted cumin powder: 1 tsp.
- Lightly roasted coriander powder: 1 tbsp.
- Cloves: 2
- Black cardamom: 1 large pod
- Dried bay leaf: 2
- Salt: 1 tbsp.
- Coconut oil: 1 tbsp.
- Water: 4 cups to soak/4 cups to cook.

COOKING INSTRUCTIONS:

1. Rinse red kidney beans thoroughly in water at least 3-4 times.
2. Soak beans in 5 cups of water overnight.
3. In the morning, switch your 3 quart slow cooker onto the low heat setting.
4. Add 1 tsp. of coconut oil and 3 cups of water. Next, throw in the soaked kidney beans along with any water that still might be left in the soaking dish.
5. Chop onion, ginger, garlic and tomatoes very finely and add them to the cooking dish.
6. Throw in all the dry ingredients as well.
7. Let it cook for 8 hours.
8. After 8 hours, check if the beans are well-cooked. They must be easy to mash with a spoon, and the rest

of the ingredients should have turned into an appetizing red-brown thick gravy.

9. Serve hot, garnished with chopped fresh coriander leaves.

This curry goes very well with rice and that will give you a totally gluten-free, soy-free, spicy, and filling lunch.

Basmati Rice

Here's how to prepare your rice in the slow cooker.

Servings: 4

Preparation time: 00H:20M:00

Cooking time: 02H:00:00

Total time: 02H:20M:00

INGREDIENTS:

- Long grain basmati rice: 1½ cups
- Salt: 1 pinch
- Cumin seeds: ½ tsp.
- Coconut oil: ½ tsp.
- Water: 3 cups

COOKING INSTRUCTIONS:

1. Wash rice under running water for a few minutes until the drained water is clear.
2. Soak rice in warm water for 10 minutes.
3. Switch on the slow cooker to the high setting.
4. Spray ½ tsp. of coconut oil all over the bottom of the cooking dish.

5. Add salt and cumin seeds, stir well.

6. Add drained rice and water.

7. Let it cook for 2 hours or more. Check after two hours to see if it is done.

8. Serve hot with curry.

Stuffed Green Peppers in Pasta Sauce

Bell peppers are a healthy choice for a light and nutritious dinner. This dish is very appetizing and looks great on the table if you are having guests over. You can always substitute green bell peppers with yellow, but the green ones will taste better when used in Indian recipes. Potatoes add to the comforting factor in this recipe while soya provides protein.

Serving: 2

Preparation time: 00H:25:00

Cooking time: 03H:20M:00

Total Time: 03H:45M:00

INGREDIENTS:

- Peppers: 4 medium-sized, red or green
- Potatoes: 1 medium-sized
- Soya granules: 1 cup
- Onion: 1 medium-sized
- Cilantro: ¼ cup
- Tomato puree: 1 cup
- Coconut oil spray
- Turmeric: 1 tsp.
- Red Chili Powder: 1/4 tsp.

- Dried mango powder: 1 tsp.
- Roasted coriander seed powder: 2 tsp.
- Roasted cumin powder: 1 tsp.
- Salt: 1 tsp.
- Water: 6 cups

COOKING INSTRUCTIONS:

1. Pour three cups of water into a pot and add potato to boil. After 15 minutes, drain the water and let the potato cool down.
2. Pour 3 cups of water into another pan and bring it to a boil. As soon as it reaches boiling temperature, throw in the soya granules. Boil for 5 minutes, then drain the water away.
3. Peel potato, break it into small pieces with a masher, and put it into a large bowl.
4. Finely chop the onion and cilantro and add it to the mashed potato.
5. Add half a teaspoon of salt and one teaspoon of coriander powder to this mixture. Keep the remainder for use in the gravy.
6. Add boiled soya granules, turmeric powder, red chili powder, dried mango powder, and roasted cumin powder to the potato mixture.

7. Take a spoon and run it through the mixture, making sure all the spices and ingredients bind well. You can check the flavor before stuffing and add more salt or chili powder per taste.

8. Wash the bell peppers thoroughly under running water.

9. Place them onto a chopping board and gently cut the top stem area into a nice round shape that can be re-used as a fancy lid once the peppers are stuffed.

10. Remove the seeds from inside the pepper. You can even wash and drain the inside to remove any seeds left inside.

11. Gently stuff the potato-soya mixture into each of the peppers until full.

12. Spray oil on the bottom of the crock pot and add ½ cup of water. Then, add tomato puree, remaining salt, and coriander powder and stir it well.

13. Place stuffed bell peppers into the sauce and make sure to put the stem lid back on each of the peppers. This will allow the flavors to stay sealed inside the pepper.

14. Set the crock pot to high.

15. Let it cook on high for 4 hours until you see that the sauce has thickened into gravy and the

peppers are fully cooked. Check the gravy for flavor. If you want to add a bit of chili powder to make it hot and spicy, do so!

16. Serve these stuffed and nutritious bell peppers warm with rice or flat bread.

Spicy Pumpkin Curry

Pumpkin is a popular Indian vegetable. Although a bit on the sweeter side, once it's cooked in a medley of Indian spices, it can be turned into a flavourful curry and coupled with flatbread for a delicious and healthy lunch or dinner. Pumpkin has high amount of Vitamins A, B, C and E, as well as minerals like potassium, copper, and manganese. With low calories, this vibrantly coloured squash provides you a great amount of fiber and a variety of antioxidants.

Servings: 2

Preparation Time: 00H:20M:00

Cooking Time: 04H:00M:00

Total time: 04H:20M:00

INGREDIENTS:

- Pumpkin: 10"x10" piece (approximate)
- Tomatoes: 3 medium-sized
- Green peas: ½ cup
- Onions: 2 medium-sized
- Garlic: 3 cloves
- Ginger: 1 inch piece
- Fresh coriander: ½ cup

- Chili powder: ¼ tsp.

- Ground black pepper: ¼ tsp.

- Salt: 1½ tbsp.

- Ground coriander seeds: 1 tbsp.

- Cumin powder: 1 tbsp.

- Dry mango powder: 1 tbsp.

- Coconut oil: 1 tbsp.

- Water: 5 cups

COOKING INSTRUCTIONS:

1. Peel the pumpkin skin with a strong knife. It can be a little hard to take the skin off. Cut the pumpkin into 1" squares. (Note: Removing the skin can be made easier by lightly steaming or roasting the pumpkin first.)

2. Grind tomatoes into a paste.

3. Wash green peas in warm water and set aside.

4. Switch on the slow cooker and set it to low. Add 1 tablespoon of coconut oil. As it heats up, throw in cumin and coriander powder. After 2 minutes, add 5 cups of water and throw in the peas, pumpkin pieces, and tomato puree.

5. Peel and finely chop onions, garlic, and ginger. Add into the cooker.

6. Add chili powder, ground pepper, salt, and dried mango powder into the cooker.

7. Let it cook for 5 hours.

8. Wash fresh coriander leaves under running water. Chop them finely.

9. When the pumpkin curry is ready, empty the slow cooker into a serving bowl, garnish with coriander leaves, and serve hot. This curry is normally eaten with flatbread called "chapatti." If you are looking for a gluten-free accompaniment, you can try Indian-style cornmeal flatbread or black millet flour flatbread.

Black Millet Flour Flatbread

Servings: 2

Preparation time: 00H:05M:00

Cooking time: 00H:40M:00

Total time: 00H:45M:00

INGREDIENTS

- Black millet flour: 4 cups
- Water: 1 cup
- Salt: ¼ tsp.
- Coconut oil: 4 tbsp.

COOKING INSTRUCTIONS

1. Knead the millet flour with water and salt into a soft dough. Millet flour doesn't bind as well as wheat flour does. It should feel like clay in your hands.
2. Heat up a skillet over a medium flame.
3. Make a round dumpling of the dough and place it in your palm. Flatten it gently to shape it into a circular bun.
4. Pour ½ tablespoon of oil into the skillet and place the circular dough in the oil. Press it gently to help it

expand into a bigger circular piece. It won't be as thin as a wrap, but shouldn't be thicker than 1.5 cm.

5. Let it cook for five minutes. Use a wide spatula to gradually flip it over to the other side. The top should be light golden brown. Wait for another five minutes until the other side is roasted. Pour ½ tbsp. of coconut oil near the sides of the flatbread. The bottom should turn into a golden brown crust. Remove it from the skillet and repeat until you have used all the dough making millet chappatis.

6. Serve hot with curry.

Palak Chana Daal

A good meal should have a balance of all the important nutrients. Palak chana daal is one such recipe that combines the goodness of green leafy vegetables with protein-rich split chick peas. Split peas are a great source of iron.

If you have a programmable slow cooker or crockpot with multiple options, you can follow this recipe as it is. A multi-cooker or programmable cooker usually gives you steam, bake, boil, and fry options. However, if you don't have a multi-cooker, you can prepare "tarka" in a frying pan and add it to the slow cooker.

Serves: 4

Preparation Time: 00H:20M:00
Cooking Time: 04H:30M:00
Total Time: 04H:50M:00

INGREDIENTS

- Spinach leaves: 2 cups
- Split chick peas (Yellow chana daal): 1 cup
- Onions: 2 medium-sized
- Ginger: 2"x2" piece
- Garlic: 4 cloves

- Tomatoes: 2 medium-sized
- Green chilies: 1 small
- Himalayan salt: 1 tbsp. (You can use regular salt too, just half the quantity)
- Cumin: 1 tsp.
- Coriander powder: 2 tsp.
- Bay leaf: 1
- Black cardamom: 1 pod
- Cloves: 3
- Coconut oil: 2 tbsp.
- Lemon: 1

COOKING INSTRUCTIONS

1. Wash split chick peas in warm water for 2-3 minutes until the drained water is clear. Soak them in warm water for 15 minutes.
2. Peel ginger, garlic, and onion. Chop finely and set aside.
3. Finely chop tomatoes and green chili and set aside. Wash spinach leaves and cut roughly in half.
4. Set up the crockpot, select the Brown/Sauté function, and keep it at medium heat. If you are using a pan, heat it over a medium flame.
5. Add 2 tablespoons of coconut oil. Let it warm for a 1-2 minutes. Throw in cumin seed, bay leaf, and cloves.

6. When the cumin starts to sizzle, add the chopped onion, garlic, and ginger mixture. Allow it to sauté for 10 minutes until the mixture is golden brown.

7. Add coriander powder and sauté for one minute.

8. Add chopped tomatoes and green chilies and cover the lid. This process is called "tarka."

9. Now add split peas, water, salt, and black cardamom. Let it cook for 4 hours at medium heat.

10. After four hours, stir it to check if the peas are well cooked and the gravy has thickened enough. If required, you can add a little more water. Whether you like thick or thin gravy depends on individual taste.

11. Add spinach leaves and let it cook for another 30 minutes.

12. Cut lemon into two halves just before you are ready to serve/eat the curry.

13. After half an hour, pour the cooked palak-chana curry into a serving bowl and drizzle a few drops of lemon juice on top. Serve hot with rice or flatbread. If you are not specifically looking for gluten-free flatbread, you could even warm up pita bread or a wheat or corn tortilla wrap.

Khichri

This is an easy, yet tasty recipe for one of those days when it's cold and windy outside and you are looking to have a comforting, warm, and "stewy" dinner. The original recipe is topped with a lot of ghee, which is a by-product of butter. However, we suggest using coconut oil instead of ghee, which keeps this meal totally vegan, nourishing, and comforting. The biggest flavour you can distinguish in this meal is ginger. Ginger is anti-inflammatory and is traditionally used to cure the cold and flu. Black pepper also strengthens immunity and relieves nasal congestion and sore throat. We have kept it lightly spiced and ideal for anyone suffering from cold-like symptoms.

Servings: 4

Preparation Time: 00H:20M:00
Cooking Time: 04H:00M:00
Total Time: 04H:20M:00

INGREDIENTS

- Green mung lentils: ¼ cup
- Rice: 1 cup
- Carrots: 1

- Ginger: 2"x2" piece
- Coconut oil: 1 tbsp.
- Himalayan salt: 1 tbsp. (You can use regular salt, just half the quantity)
- Black pepper: 1 tsp.
- Black cardamom: 1 pod
- Cloves: 3
- Cumin powder: 1 tsp.
- Coriander powder: 1 tbsp.
- Mint leaves: 6
- Water: 4 cups

COOKING INSTRUCTIONS

1. Wash mung lentils thoroughly under warm running water and leave them to soak for 15 minutes in warm water.
2. Wash rice in running water until the drained water comes out clear. Set it aside.
3. Set the slow cooker to high heat.
4. Add a tablespoon of coconut oil. After about 10 minutes, as the oil warms up, add cumin seeds and let them fry. After 20 minutes, the seeds will start to sizzle.
5. Meanwhile, remove the skin of the ginger and chop finely. Peel the upper skin of the carrot, grate it, and set

aside. You could even buy ready-to-use grated carrots from the grocery store.

6. Add mung beans, rice, and chopped ginger along with all of the dry ingredients except mint leaves. Leave the mint for the last minute.

7. After cooking for 4 hours, you will notice that the rice and mung beans are all cooked in a starchy kind of stew with light orange carrot floating around. Switch off the slow cooker.

8. Add mint leaves and put the lid back on. Leave it for another half an hour.

9. Serve it warm. It can be eaten by itself, no breads required. But if you would like choose gluten-free or regular bread, toast it to have a crunchier addition to your dinner.

10. Feel free to add more salt and pepper if you feel the stew needs it.

Pulav

This recipe is great for a multi-programmable slow cooker or crock pot because you can complete the entire cooking process in the same container. If you don't have one, though, do not worry. Simply warm some oil in a pan and sauté the dry ingredients and onions for 3-5 minutes, then add them into the rice before you start cooking.

Servings: 4

Preparation Time: 00H:25M:00
Cooking Time: 02H:10M:00
Total Time: 02H:35M:00

INGREDIENTS

- Long grain Basmati rice: 1½ cup
- Water: 3 cups
- Carrots: 1 medium-sized
- Green bell pepper: 1 medium-sized
- Green beans: 10
- White mushrooms: 4
- Onions: 2 medium-sized

- Himalayan salt: 1 tbsp. (You can use regular salt, just half the quantity)
- Cumin: 1 tsp.
- Coriander powder: 2 tsp.
- Red chili powder: ¼ tsp.
- Ground black pepper: ¼ tsp.
- Bay leaf: 1
- Black cardamom: 1 pod
- Star anise: 1
- Cloves: 1
- Cinnamon: ¼ stick
- Coconut oil: 2 tbsp.

COOKING INSTRUCTION

1. Wash the rice under running water for 2-3 minutes until the water runs clear. Let the rice soak in clean, warm water for 10 minutes.
2. Meanwhile, chop carrots, green peppers, beans, and mushrooms. Set aside.
3. Slice the onions into halves. Rest the onion with the cut side down on the chopping board. With a sharp knife, slice along the lines of longitude, from top end to root end. Slice both the onions in this manner and keep them in a bowl.
4. Warm up your multi-cooker and set it to brown/sauté. Add 2 tablespoons of coconut oil and cumin seeds. When

the seeds begin to sizzle, add finely sliced onions and sauté for 3 minutes while stirring occasionally. Add coriander powder and continue to brown for another 30 seconds. Add bay leaf, black cardamom, cloves, and star anise.

5. Switch off the brown/sauté function. Cover with the lid.

6. Switch the cooking function to boil on high heat. Add the chopped vegetables, salt, and red chili powder.

7. Drain rice carefully and pour into the slow cooker. Add three cups of water and stir well. Let it cook for two hours.

8. Most cookers have a timer for rice. Check to see if yours has one. Some slow cookers can cook any kind of rice within 15 minutes. A regular slow cooker should take 1½-2 hours.

9. Make sure the rice is well-cooked (inflated and softened grain) and also make sure that the vegetables are done. If they are not, leave it to cook in its steam for another 15 minutes.

10. Your vegan, soy-free, sugar-free, and gluten-free pulav is ready to be eaten!

11. Indians would traditionally add some pickled mango or lemon to go with the pulav. Indian pickles are vegan and gluten-free, too!

Gajar Ka Halwa

If you have had the chance to attend an Indian wedding or any grand feast, you may have been served this sweet and rich carrot pudding. We, vegans would have skipped it since most of these puddings are cooked in milk and milk products. But this recipe is a vegan Indian carrot pudding recipe which you can cook in your crock pot! We can always make something similar our way, the gluten-free, vegan way!

Servings: 8

Preparation Time: 00H:45M:00
Cooking Time: 05H:00M:00
Total Time: 05H:45M:00

INGREDIENTS:

- Carrots: 8 medium-sized (1 lb.)
- Almond milk: 6 cups
- Coconut oil: 2 tbsp.
- Dried coconut: 2"x2" piece
- Almonds: 6
- Raisins: ¼ cup
- Coconut or brown sugar: 1/4 cup
- Cardamom: 5 pods
- Cinnamon powder: ½ tsp

- Pistachios: 2 tbsp.

COOKING INSTRUCTIONS:

1. Start by washing and peeling the carrots.
2. Rinse the carrots let them dry a bit. Grate these carrots by hand, or if you have a food processor, it can grate the carrots finely for you. We don't recommend buying grated carrots from the store as they are typically thicker and do not give the same texture and taste when cooked.
3. Grate the dried coconut piece and set aside. Grind cardamom into a powder.
4. Chop pistachios and almond into small pieces.
5. Set your slow cooker to the medium setting. Add one tablespoon of coconut oil.
6. Add grated carrots and coconut in the cooker and stir them to coat them in the oil. Add almond milk, ground cardamom, and cinnamon powder.
7. Let it cook for three hours.
8. Add sugar and stir to combine. Continue cooking for another two hours.
9. Add almonds. Switch off the cooker.
10. Heat a frying pan over a medium flame on the stove. Add one tablespoon of coconut oil.
11. Once the oil heats up, add raisins and sauté for 30 seconds.

12. Empty the contents of the cooker into the pan and stir well. Make sure there is no almond milk left. Keep stirring on medium flame until the milk has evaporated and the carrots are well-cooked and sautéed.

13. How to recognize that the carrots are sautéed: Indian guidelines ask that the sautéed ingredients start pulling away from the bottom of the pan or pot that they are being cooked in. They will not stick to the pan or pot, and the oil will begin to separate from the sauté. If you don't see the oil separating from the contents and pulling away from the bottom, continue to stir-fry.

14. Serve hot or cold as you like. Garnish with chopped pistachios on top.

Free eBook with Vegan Smoothie Recipes!

Before you go, I would like to offer you a free, complimentary eBook + free newsletter that goes with it (with even more information about vegan recipes).

We are in this together!

Simply visit:

www.yourwellnessbooks.com/karen-smoothies to grab your free copy!

In case you happen to have any technical problems- email me at:

karenveganbooks@gmail.com

and I will be happy to help!

Thank you again for taking an interest in my work. I hope you will enjoy this bonus!

More Books by Karen Greenvang (aka Karen Vegan) available in your local Amazon store!

Just search for "Karen Greenvang".

Enjoy!